GLENEAGLES
TO
GLASTONBURY

STEAM IN THE THIRTIES

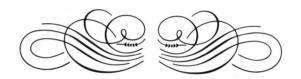

Dr. Ian Allen

Oxford Publishing Co

ISBN 0-86093-351-2

Typesetting by:
Aquarius Typesetting Services, New Milton, Hants.

Printed in Great Britain by:
Netherwood Dalton & Co. Ltd., Huddersfield, Yorks.

Published by:
Oxford Publishing Co.
Link House
West Street
POOLE, Dorset

Preface

'That could only have been an elephant' I said to my brother. 'Don't be silly' he replied, 'elephants don't roam the streets of Reading on Sunday afternoons'. The 1923 model Austin 7 in which we were travelling had just skidded a full circle through 360 degrees and had then continued its journey as if nothing had happened. But I was right; we turned a corner, and there ahead was the elephant. It was a beautiful beast and was going to the station to take the train to its next destination, together with all the other circus animals.

It was 1933. Cars in the 1920s had been rich men's prerogatives. In the early 1930s many second and third-hand machines were coming on to the market in increasing numbers. Providing you were 18 years old, you could obtain a driving licence without any test; a kind friend gave you one or two lessons and then you drove off to where your fancy took you.

The week I bought my first car was that in which petrol was reduced to 1s. 3d. (6p) a gallon. There were no continuous white or yellow lines, no traffic wardens and no MOT tests. The cream of the railway traffic had begun to go by road in increasing quantities since the general strike of 1926, but all the local goods yards were still full, and every day the local freight train would arrive, and for an hour or two there would be the clanging of trucks being shunted up and down. Cycling was always enjoyable. Places like Hanger Lane, Ealing (where my father was taken as a boy to hear the nightingales), the North Circular road (what there was of it), and the Elephant & Castle and Vauxhall, with its tramcars, could all be navigated without difficulty or delay.

Dr.Beeching (as he subsequently became) was as yet a young unknown man. My brother and I grew up overlooking the railway line. We had no need for clocks or watches — wherever we might be in the house, we knew exactly which train was passing or even, in the case of the local locomotives, the number of the locomotive. Every locomotive had a slightly different note. When we had finally saved up enough money for a bicycle, the local station was the first ride we took. When my godmother gave me a small Brownie box camera for my birthday, I deserted her, forthwith, and again went straight to the local station to take my first railway photographs.

Up to the passing of steam in 1968, there were few boys whose favourite toy, at one time or another, had not been a clockwork engine. For a year or two these were replaced, half-heartedly, by tractors — but no boy ever had as much ambition to be a tractor driver as he had to be an engine driver. Curiously, as trains disappeared for the boys, so did dolls for their sisters.

As we grew up we cycled more and more round the countryside, finding aged locomotives to photograph and branch lines to explore. Bed and breakfast was only 3s. 6d. (17½p) a night (for members of the Cycling Tourist Club it was 4s. 6d.), but to cycle 100 miles or so to see a particularly interesting train took time, and with professional exams beginning to loom on the horizon, time was becoming more and more precious. So when we were suddenly left £10 in an aged relative's will, it became possible to buy a car.

Thus it happened that we were returning from Oxford through Reading on that particular Sunday afternoon. It was always an adventure to go out in the 'Baby Austin'. With a following wind it would average 47 miles to the gallon, and against a strong head wind it would do 43. With our limited available cash we had to decide how much petrol it would require to get us home and then spend the rest of our money on food and drink. On one occasion we miscalculated the strength of the headwind on the Great North Road, and ran out of petrol in the middle of Trafalgar Square in the rush hour. I can still remember the feeling of power that came over me when I got out of the car and surveyed the traffic havoc that I had wrought (and, incidentally, heard many new words!). When we came to a steep hill, the car had to be run backwards into the bank while the passengers alighted — the brakes would not hold on a gradient. After turning the car, once in reverse it would tackle anything. Nobody thought this method of climbing the least bit odd.

The coming of the cheap car, although it so swiftly broke the century-old railway monopoly of transport, coincided with less expensive photography. Up to the 1920s, railway photography had been for the few, requiring a great deal of equipment. One of the great railway photographers at this time used to take with him a half plate camera with glass slides, a tripod and a chair to stand on when he went out on a railway photographic expedition. He used to say that to get a good photograph the eye must be on a level with the centre line of the boiler. His results were outstanding.

However, the average photographer had still to be content with the simplest of equipment. All the photographs in this book were taken with a 3¼in. x 2¼in. roll film camera, a film speed of ASA64, a maximum shutter speed of 1/250th of a second and a maximum lens aperture of f6.3. I had no lens hood or exposure meter, but a Zeiss lens was essential to get the necessary definition. A knowledge of map reading was one of the most useful things learnt at school.

This was the background of the photographs I have put together in this book. Except for about half a dozen, most were taken between 1930 and 1935. Looking through my album, with hindsight, these were probably the most fascinating years in the history of the steam locomotive. There were still large numbers of very elderly pre-grouping examples working in 1930. By 1935, many of these had been withdrawn in the interests of standardisation, and had been replaced by modern standard types. The first experimental diesel was introduced in 1931 — by 1935 several were at work, indicating what lay ahead.

Finally, there must be many people today who are somewhat bewildered by the infinite variety of locomotives that were at work fifty years ago. I have tried to show the origin and development of some of these. A good photographic outing could produce at least a dozen different types — so very different from today.

DEDICATION

To my brother, George, my companion and navigator for most
of the time whilst taking the photographs shown in this book.

Plate 1: Pride of place in this book must be given to this picture of the 'Royal Scot' express, the 10a.m. Euston to Glasgow, bursting out of Watford Tunnel in June 1934, on its 300 mile non-stop journey to Carlisle. The train is hauled by LMS 3-cylinder 4-6-0 No. 6100 *Royal Scot* which had recently returned from its triumphant 1933 tour of America and Canada. For this it had been fitted with the regulation bell on the smokebox. The load was 16 coaches weighing, loaded, not less than 550 tons. *Royal Scot* is now preserved at Bressingham in Norfolk, where Dick Allen, a retired top link driver from Camden, who often drove the Royal train on its journeys from Euston, used to give rides on its footplate. He said he had no favourite locomotive. Most of all he enjoyed one which was being difficult and he loved rising to a challenge. If all was not well on the footplate at Watford, he was determined that he would bring his train into Carlisle on time, and that the locomotive would do what he wished.

Plate 2: This shows an ex-London, Brighton & South Coast Railway 'Terrier' 0-6-0T on the Kent & East Sussex Railway, and was taken a few months after the previous photograph — a greater contrast could not be imagined. The locomotive, No. 3, built at Brighton in 1872, is propelling its train of one 4-wheeled ex-LSWR coach weighing, at the most, about eight tons, up from Rolvendon to Tenterden. During 1933/4, a fitter from the Brighton Works of the Southern Railway used to come over to Rolvendon at the weekends and, with some local manual help, completely rebuilt No. 3, using parts off another 'Terrier', No. 5, which had been bought in January 1905. It was at this time it acquired its unique bunker. In 1943, it was fitted with a second-hand Southern Railway boiler, and at the time of writing (1985), aged 113 years, it is again back at work after a major overhaul. For the author it was the fulfilment of a life-long ambition to travel in a first class Pullman car, when No. 3 hauled a 'Dine and Wine' train conveying first class Pullman car *Barbara* over the preserved Kent & East Sussex line. In the 1930s, the Kent & East Sussex Railway had an even older coach than the one shown in the photograph. This was an ex-Royal saloon of 1848, and even on the rough K&ESR track, it rode beautifully. The last train on the Hayling Island branch, a society special, was hauled in November 1963 by two 91 year old 'Terriers', Nos. 32636 and 32670. This must be something of a record. After nationalisation K&ESR No. 3 became BR No. 32670.

Plate 3: As I have said in my preface, the fascination of the railways in the early 1930s was the wonderful mixture of old and new. World War I and then the Grouping of 1923 had prolonged the lives of many of the old — the advent of the new could not be put off any longer. The new is shown in *Plate 1* with the 'Royal Scot' hauling sixteen coaches — the old could not be shown better than by this picture of LMS 'Jumbo' class 2-4-0 No. 5014 *Murdock* seen entering Northampton on a local train in 1931. *Murdoch* was built by John Ramsbotham in 1866; it was completely renewed by Francis Webb in 1888. The most famous 'Jumbo' is *Hardwicke*, now preserved in the National Railway Museum, York. The 'Jumbos' survived into the new era with the building of the two LMS Pacifics, *Princess Royal* and *Princess Elizabeth*, in 1933. They were strongly built, with a free steaming boiler and short steam passages, and were completely reliable, which is more than the many varieties of Compounds built by Francis Webb in the 1880s and 1890s, and which his successor, George Whale, soon withdrew.

Very early in the development of English locomotives, three principal types emerged. These were 2-2-2 single wheelers for express passenger trains, 2-4-0s for traffic requiring greater adhesion, and 0-6-0s for freight.

In Scotland, where there were many lightly-laid colliery lines with sharp curves, 0-4-2 locomotives became very popular, particularly on the Caledonian and Glasgow & South Western railways. Patrick Stirling, who had been appointed Chief Mechanical Engineer to the G&SWR at Kilmarnock in 1853, took the type with him when he was appointed Chief Mechanical Engineer to the GNR at Doncaster in 1866. Between 1867 and 1895, he built 154 examples, all with 5ft. 7in. driving wheels, the last 33 having slightly larger cylinders. Stirling soon found that the severe gradients of West Yorkshire required the greater adhesion of an 0-6-0, but he preferred his 0-4-2s for mixed traffic duties until his retirement in 1895.

The GWR built some small 0-4-2 tanks in the late 1860s, which were rebuilt to conform with the very long-lived 517 class, but the 0-4-2s in England will always be associated with William Stroudley.

William Stroudley was born in 1833, and by the age of ten he had left school and was working with his father. Such was his remarkable genius that in 1870, aged 37, he was appointed Chief Mechanical Engineer to the London, Brighton & South Coast Railway.

In 1872, he built the first of his famous 'Terrier' class 0-6-0 tanks *(see Plate 2)*, followed in 1873 by the Class D1 0-4-2 tanks, of which 125 were subsequently built, and in 1874 by the Class E1 0-6-0 tanks, which were largely standard with the D1s.

His front-coupled Class D1 tanks were so successful that the type had developed, by 1882, into his 6ft. 6in. front-coupled Gladstones *(compare Plate 3)*.

Plate 4: This shows a Gladstone class 0-4-2 locomotive, Southern Railway No. B194, standing at Brighton Station in 1930. The first of the class, No. 214 *Gladstone*, is now preserved at the National Railway Museum, York. The disadvantage of the front-coupled 0-4-2 type was that any further development was restricted. The orthodox 2-4-0 could be developed into the 4-4-0, of which the Southern Railway's 'Schools' class is a supreme example *(see Plate 36)*.

Plate 5: At Derby, locomotive design had followed the usual English development. Matthew Kirtley was appointed as the first Chief Mechanical Engineer in 1844. He was born in 1812 and is said to have driven the first train up from Birmingham, hitting the buffer stops at Euston. Many of his locomotives had very long lives. It is astonishing that it was possible, in 1933, to photograph an express train hauled by a 2-4-0 built in 1868 (to an 1867 design), piloting a 4-4-0 which was built in 1886. This view shows LMS 2-4-0 No. 19 (pilot) and LMS 4-4-0 No. 369 (train locomotive). No. 369 had been rebuilt with a larger non-superheated boiler. The train is a north to west express and is pictured near Cheltenham on the Derby to Bristol main line. The coach next to the locomotive is one of the very distinctive Wolverton-built LNWR 12-wheeled dining cars — a superb example of British railway craftsmanship. Samuel Johnson succeeded Matthew Kirtley in 1873 and retired in 1903. He had designed the first English wide cylinder 4-4-0 at Stratford (London) for the Great Eastern Railway, and in the 1870s and 1880s, at Derby, designed large numbers of 2-4-0s and 4-4-0s, side by side.

Plate 6 (top right): Another remarkable survivor from the past is shown here; Southern Railway 2-4-0T No. 3329. This locomotive was built in 1875 to a design dating back to the 1850s, and was the last of a class of 85 built for the LSWR by Joseph Beattie, between 1863 and 1875. The first withdrawal of one of this class was in 1886, and by 1898 all had gone except three which were retained to work the Wenford Bridge china clay line in North Cornwall. These three were not withdrawn until 1962. One is now preserved in working order at Quainton Road. From the earliest days of railways, all the timetables were collected together into a monthly volume, and were called *Bradshaw* after the editor. *Bradshaw* quickly became an English institution. No hostess could be without a copy for the convenience of her guests, and it became fashionable for people to plan imaginary journeys such as Gleneagles to Glastonbury (this was before the days of Bridge and television). From a study of *Bradshaw* in the 1930s it transpired that on alternate Mondays only there was a passenger train from Wadebridge to Bodmin. It seemed quite possible that this train might be hauled by one of the legendary 2-4-0 tank engines. There was not the railway information available in those days that there is today. To be at Wadebridge in the early hours of an alternate Monday was not easy, but my brother and I finally accomplished it, and it was a tremendous moment of triumph when the locomotive came round the bend. Our guess had been right — it was hauled by a 2-4-0 tank. These archaic locomotives continued to work on occasional passenger trains until their withdrawal in 1962.

Plate 7 (right): Southern Railway Gladstone class 0-4-2 No. B172 is pictured in October 1932 with an Ashford to Brighton train at London Road, Brighton. No. B172 was the last Gladstone to be built, and the last to be withdrawn, in 1933. In the summer of 1933, No. B172 used to arrive at London (Victoria) from Tunbridge Wells, usually on a Friday, and could be seen standing side by side with the newly-introduced Brighton electrics.

Plate 8: In this view, Southern Railway 0-4-2 locomotive No. 632 is seen with a Waterloo to Alton train at Bentley. In the bay is Drummond 0-4-4 tank No. 128 with a Bordon push and pull branch train. Ninety mixed traffic 0-4-2s with 6ft. driving wheels were built by W. Adams for the LSWR between 1887 and 1895. They proved to be very successful. One of the class, No. 555, achieved immortal fame by hauling Queen Victoria's funeral train between Gosport and Fareham in 1901. This photograph makes an interesting comparison with Stroudley's express 0-4-2 shown in *Plate 7.*

Plate 9 (top right): Mention was made in *Plate 5* of Samuel Johnson's inside cylinder 4-4-0s, and their subsequent rebuilding. It was still possible, in the 1930s, to find unrebuilt examples of this type working on the Midland & Great Northern Railway. Here they performed tremendous feats of haulage, both on the very heavy holiday trains, between the Midlands and East Anglia, and on the freight trains which served the fertile Fenlands. Originally there had been 33 locomotives of this type built between 1894 and 1899 for the M&GN. Of these, 10 had been rebuilt with larger non-superheated Derby boilers, but the remaining 23 remained very much in their original condition, except that all were fitted with extended smokeboxes, and some had small standard Belpaire boilers. A Johnson M&GN 4-4-0, No. 3, is pictured near Mundesley, working a Cromer Beach to Yarmouth Beach train.

Plate 10 (bottom right): When Stroudley died in 1889, he was succeeded as Chief Mechanical Engineer by R. J. Billinton. The latter had been at Brighton with Stroudley before being promoted chief draughtsman to Samuel Johnson. It was natural, therefore, that Billinton's initial designs should be based on Derby practice. His first design was a Midland type 0-4-4T, built in 1892, his second, a Midland type 0-6-0, built in 1893 and his third, a very small Midland type 4-4-0, built in 1895. The latter were not so powerful as the Derby type 4-4-0s built in 1894 for the Midland & Great Northern Railway, as their boilers proved too small. The whole class was subsequently rebuilt with a larger standard Marsh boiler. One of these rebuilt 4-4-0 locomotives, SR Class B2X 4-4-0 No. B316, is pictured passing Leatherhead with a 'down' London Bridge to Portsmouth train. For their entire life they were associated with the Mid-Sussex line. An interesting reason for the survival of Class B2X locomotives, Nos. B206 and B315 for several years after the rest of the class had been withdrawn, was that they were required to work an 'up' morning train from Portsmouth which ran to London Bridge, via Horsham and Three Bridges. The Class L11 LSWR 4-4-0s which had taken over the Fratton duties, used to become derailed on the curve leading out of Horsham towards Three Bridges, so could not be used on this route. Nos. B206 and B315 survived until after the Brighton electrification in 1933. The Brighton boiler shop always had an excellent reputation, and the standard boilers off Billinton's Class B2X 4-4-0s were used again on the Class C2X 0-6-0s, some surviving until the end of steam at Brighton in 1962.

Plate 11 (top left): At Brighton, Billinton was quickly forced to reconsider his small engine policy, which he had brought from Derby, and in 1899, he produced a much larger locomotive, of which SR 4-4-0 Class B4, No. 2049, is an example. No. 2049 is shown hauling a very heavy load, for this route, of 324 tons empty, with an 'up' Portsmouth to London Bridge, via West Croydon, express near Ford Junction.

Plate 12 (bottom left): SR Class B4 4-4-0, No. B74, is seen working a 'down' Brighton race special composed of Billinton 6-wheeled coaches. The bodies of these coaches were soon to be placed on steel underframes, to form coaches for the next phase of the Southern Railway suburban electrification. Two trains of clerestory bogies were borrowed from the GWR during 1927/8 to cover the conversion, and were mainly used on the London to Worthing service. After World War I, the Brighton Railway was very short of rolling stock and, at busy times, repaired coaches were sent back into traffic without being repainted; this led to some very piebald effects. As late as 1926, the Epsom to Waterloo workmen's train, composed of LSWR six wheelers, came up the main line, on one occasion, non-stop from Andover to Waterloo, via East Putney. Travel in 6-wheeled vehicles was always exhilarating as these coaches gave an enhanced sensation of speed, especially on sections of 30ft. rail. The wires for the overhead electric suburban trains, introduced by the LB&SCR are well-shown in this view.

Plate 13: Modern superheaters first came into use in 1908, and they were a great advance in the history of the development of the steam locomotive. Billinton Class B4 4-4-0, No. B46, which was fitted with a superheated boiler in 1916, is seen on an 'up' Newhaven boat express passing Salfords Halt in 1932. The Pullman car is one of the old American-built cars and has a clerestory. Newhaven and Eastbourne locomotives were always magnificently kept during the years between the wars.

Plate 14: After World War I, increased power was urgently needed by the LB&SCR for the London to Portsmouth services, which were being heavily taxed by the small Class B2X 4-4-0s, about a dozen of which were stationed at Fratton for these services *(see Plate 10).* In 1922, twelve Class B4 4-4-0s were therefore rebuilt with larger Class K boilers, some of which were constructed at Derby. Owing to the difficult post-war conditions, the original front end arrangement had to be retained, and this limited the piston valves to 8in. diameter. These engines did their best work on the Mid-Sussex route, for which they were designed. On heavy trains on the steeply-graded line from London to Horsham, with its many severe service slacks, their work was indistinguishable from the Atlantics, although their coal consumption was always high due to their cramped front ends. I can remember being told at Brighton Works, in 1924, that this heavy coal consumption had been a disappointment. After fifty years of electric service, I do not think it is appreciated today how heavily-graded were so many of the Brighton suburban lines. SR Class B4X rebuilt 4-4-0 No. 2073 is shown on a Sunday New Cross to Bournemouth through train, near Amberley.

Plate 15: The first British inside cylinder 4-4-0s to be fitted with an adequate boiler, were built at St. Rollox in 1896 for the Caledonian Railway and were called the 'Dunalastair' class. After its immediate success, nearly all the other lines followed suit, and S. W. Johnson, in 1900, built a much larger 4-4-0 which was known as a Class 3. One of these Class 3 4-4-0s, No. 763, piloted by a Class 2 4-4-0, No. 557, is seen on an 'up' slow working near Sharnbrook.

Plate 16: Towards the end of his career, in 1901, Johnson built the first Derby 3-cylinder Compound 4-4-0. The prototype Compound had been designed by W. M. Smith, who was William Worsdell's chief draughtsman at the Darlington Works of the North Eastern Railway. He had applied it to North Eastern Railway 4-4-0 No. 1619, but, regrettably, he died before his invention had been fully appreciated. I have never seen it stated how it was that S. W. Johnson took up W. M. Smith's design and immediately built a successful Compound locomotive — something that had eluded Francis Webb at Crewe for over twenty years. This photograph, taken in 1933, shows a typical Midland Railway express train climbing Sharnbrook Bank, and might have been taken any time over a period of 25 years from 1910-35. The train locomotive is an LMS Compound 4-4-0, No. 1060, and the pilot is a Class 2 LMS rebuilt 4-4-0, No. 549. The first five Compounds were built by Johnson and the next forty, to a modified design, by R. M. Deeley who succeeded Johnson. The Class 2 4-4-0s were, technically, rebuilds of Johnson's small-boilered 4-4-0s but, in reality, were totally new locomotives (like the 'Jumbos' on the LNWR already mentioned) dating from 1910. On the formation of the LMS in 1923, the Class 2 4-4-0 and Compounds were taken as standard types, and multiplied for use all over the system. I have never seen a full lay appreciation of the Compound locomotives. It would be most interesting to have details of their everyday working on the LMS, their costs, repair bills, coal and water consumption etc., and how they compared with the Class 2s.

Plate 18 (top right): LMS standard 4-4-0 No. 654, leaves Luffenham with a Peterborough East to Rugby train. The last two coaches of LMS origin are working through from Parkeston Quay to Birmingham. The through coaches, for most of their existence, were of LNER origin, and took the direct route via Wansford. When Stroudley took over from his predecessor, John Craven, he found 233 locomotives at Brighton, consisting of 72 different classes; never can there have been such a golden age for the railway photographer. Stroudley immediately initiated a policy of rigorous standardisation, which was continued by his successors.

The following five photographs *(Plates 19 to 23)* illustrate how this policy was adopted at Brighton, to meet the ever growing demand for more powerful locomotives without the expense of building new locomotives.

During 1922/3, twelve of the Class B4 4-4-0, of 1899 design, were fitted with large standard K class 2-6-0 boilers *(see Plates 12 & 14)*.

The twelve original boilers, plus six off the non-superheated Class I3 tanks, and two or three newly-built, were then fitted to Marsh's Class I1 4-4-2 tanks (D. Earle Marsh had succeeded R. J. Billinton in 1904). With their 4ft. 3in. standard boilers, the Class I1 4-4-2 tanks had proved to be too small for the work for which they were designed. The small standard 4ft. 3in. boilers off the Class I1s were then added to the pool of boilers for Classes C2, D3, E3, E4, E5 and E6.

When the large-boilered Class B4X 4-4-0s were withdrawn, their boilers were added to the pool for the Class K 2-6-0s.

Plate 19: Class I1 4-4-2T No. B5, fitted with its original 4ft. 3in. boiler, is pictured on an 'up' Brighton to London Bridge slow working near Salfords Halt.

Plate 20: Class I1X 4-4-2T No. 2002 is fitted with the large Class B4 boiler made redundant when the B4s were rebuilt. No. 2002, as built, was similar to Class I1, No. B5, shown in *Plate 19*. No. 2002 is working an 'up' Tunbridge Wells train, near Dormans.

Plate 22 (opposite): BR Class B4X 4-4-0 No. S2060 is seen working a Brighton to Bournemouth train. The photograph was taken near Brockenhurst and the train is composed of LSWR corridor coaches. For the first month or two after nationalisation in 1948 locomotives passing through the Works were not renumbered into a general series but were given a prefix. In the case of the Southern Railway this was 'S'. After withdrawal in 1951, the boiler of No. S2060 was transferred to a Class K 2-6-0.

Plate 21: Class E4 0-6-2T No. 2501, with a standard 4ft. 3in. boiler, climbs Falmer Bank with a train of Kentish coal for the locomotive depot at Brighton. When the LB&SCR became part of the Southern Railway in 1923, out of its 620 locomotives, no fewer than 248 had, at some time in their career, carried a 4ft. 3in. standard boiler.

Plate 23: Class K 2-6-0 No. 32343 is pictured on a van train at Lewes in June 1962. Its brake pipe hoses are whitewashed, indicating that three days earlier it had stood as pilot for the Derby Day Royal train on the Tattenham Corner branch. No. 32343 is fitted with the automatic warning system, and it was finally withdrawn in December 1962.

The South Eastern & Chatham Railway will always be associated with James Stirling's domeless locomotives. He succeeded his brother Patrick as Chief Mechanical Engineer at the G&SWR Works at Kilmarnock, in 1866, when his brother took up a similar appointment at Doncaster. At Kilmarnock, in 1873, he introduced his domeless 4-4-0s, the first inside cylinder examples in the country except for two at Cowlairs by Wheatley in 1871, one of which went down in the Tay Bridge disaster. Samuel Johnson's two 4-4-0s, designed at Stratford for the GER, were not actually built until after he had left for Derby.

James Stirling went to Ashford in 1878, and in 1880 he built twelve small 4-4-0s with 6ft. driving wheels. In 1883, he turned out the first of his SER Class F domeless 7ft. 4-4-0s, which were very similar to those built for the G&SWR ten years earlier. Eighty eight of this class had been built by 1898, by which time they were all outstripped by the main line demands. In this case, Sir Nigel Gresley, at one time Chief Mechanical Engineer of the GNR and subsequently the LNER, was right when he once said 'standardisation is stagnation'.

Twenty nine similar 4-4-0s with slightly enlarged boilers were built in 1898, classified B, but they showed little improvement. In 1903, rebuilding of the Fs and Bs began, when they were fitted with the standard Ashford 4ft. 4in. boiler. This was an excellent boiler influenced by Surtees, the chief draughtsman, who had come from Longhedge, the headquarters of the London, Chatham & Dover Railway. By 1920, seventy six Class F locomotives had been rebuilt to Class F1. Twenty seven Class B 4-4-0s were also fitted with similar boilers to form Class B1. The latter class always retained their larger tenders.

Plate 24: SR Class F1 rebuilt Stirling 4-4-0 No. 1060 is seen with a Reading to Brighton Sunday excursion train near Bramley, on the Guildford to Christ's Hospital branch of the LB&SCR. These trains normally reversed at Horsham where locomotives were changed. The first film of *The Railway Children* was taken at this site, in the mid-1930s but it was the second film, about thirty years later, that highlighted the universal appeal of steam trains.

Plate 25: Class D 4-4-0, No. 1733, built in 1901 after the amalgamation in 1899 of the South Eastern Railway and the London, Chatham & Dover Railway, is pictured with a 'down' train crossing the viaduct near Upper Warlingham. The rivalry between these two lines had nearly bled them to death in the 1880s and 1890s. Harry Wainwright was appointed Locomotive & Carriage Superintendent of the new SECR at Ashford in 1899. As has been stated, prolonged standardisation of obsolescent types had brought stagnation to Ashford. The influence upon new locomotive construction was predominantly Surtees', and the Class D engines were typical, strong and large-boilered, basically similar to those which most railway companies were now building, following the success of the Caledonian Railway's 'Dunalastairs'. The Class Ds were followed in 1906 by Class E 4-4-0s, and these had Belpaire fireboxes and driving wheels of 6ft. 6in. as against the 6ft. 9in. of the Ds.

Plate 26 (top right): An SR 6ft. 6in. Class E 4-4-0, No. A514, is pictured on a Tattenham Corner race special, passing Smitham.

Plate 27 (bottom right): Beginning in 1919, twenty one Class D locomotives and five Class E locomotives were rebuilt to Class D1 and Class E1 by R. Maunsell, who had been appointed Chief Mechanical Engineer at Ashford in 1913. These highly successful rebuilds will always be associated with the names of H. Holcroft, who joined Maunsell's team at Ashford, from Swindon, and James Clayton who joined from Derby, to become chief draughtsman. A Southern Railway Class E1, No. 1497, is seen on an 'up' Margate express near Fawkham Junction, and shows the striking similarity in external outline to the rebuilt Johnson 4-4-0s of the Midland Railway. Classes D1 and E1 were almost identical except for the size of their driving wheels. In 1914, the Class E 4-4-0s were developed into the larger Maunsell Class Ls, and in 1926 the Class Ls were further developed into Class L1.

Plate 28: SR Class L 4-4-0 No. 1773 recovers from a signal check at Fawkham Junction while working the 3.15p.m. 'down' Victoria to Margate express in 1932 — the most important train of the day for this route.

Plate 29: This photograph, taken a few years later, shows Class L 4-4-0 No. 1761 on a Midlands to Eastbourne and Hastings, via Brighton, through train, near Lewes. The load is a prodigious one of 13 bogies — 10 LMS and 3 local SR coaches attached at Brighton. It will be noticed that No. 1761 has acquired a Maunsell chimney and Ross safety valves.

Plate 30: When working hard, a Class L gave a magnificent roar, and these locomotives were acoustically at their best on the main line to Hastings and on the Folkestone 80 minute expresses, where they had to be worked all-out to maintain time. They were replaced on the latter trains in 1926 by the new modified Class L1 4-4-0s, the type seen in this view, which shows Class L1 4-4-0 No. 1756 leaving Sevenoaks Tunnel, with a 'down' slow train. If only there had been tape recorders in those days! The modern types of locomotives were much quieter.

William Adams, who became Chief Mechanical Engineer of the LSWR in 1878, at the age of 55, was an engineer who had come on to the rail scene by building the new Bow Works of the North London Railway in the 1850s, and had stayed on as Chief Mechanical Engineer. Here he designed two classes of very long-lived 4-4-0 tank engines. The first class to be built in 1865 was fitted with inside cylinders, and the second, in 1868, had outside cylinders. An example of a North London Railway 0-6-0 tank, the first of which was built in 1879 by Adam's successor, Mr Park, is fortunately preserved on the Bluebell Railway.

The 4-4-0 tank design, that was used so much on London's long forgotten steam services on the Underground, was originally designed by Craven, Stroudley's predecessor at Brighton, in 1859. In 1862, Beyer Peacock of Manchester built some very similar locomotives for a Spanish railway and then, in 1864, the first of many for the Metropolitan Railway.

Plate 31: London Transport 4-4-0 tank No. 23 is pictured leaving Brill in 1935 with a mixed train for Quainton Road. No. 23 was built by Beyer Peacock of Manchester in 1867. A tow rope for intermediate shunting can be seen on the front buffer beam between the two cylinders. No. 23 is now preserved in Covent Garden Museum. I shall never forget a footplate journey I once had the pleasure of making as a boy on No. 23. The motion was fascinating — a gentle fore and aft oscillation combined simultaneously with one from side to side. The driver began to tell me about his gastric ulcer which had just been cured in hospital. I had never heard of such things before, and I was so fascinated that I went home determined to be a doctor. Whenever I go to see No. 23, I always remember, with gratitude, the kindess of that driver, some fifty years ago. By a curious coincidence, the first patient I had at St. Thomas' Hospital, in my student days, was a locomotive driver from Reading, who was also suffering from a gastric ulcer. He had been a fireman on the Southern Railway 'River' class 2-6-4 tanks. One of these locomotives came off the rails at Sevenoaks and crashed into a bridge abutment and many lives were lost. The outside cylinder 4-4-0 developed much earlier than the inside cylinder type, especially in America. In 1860, Darlington produced two fine examples of the latter, with very large cabs, to give the drivers some protection from the weather on journeys over the Pennines from Darlington to Tebay. These cabs proved unpopular and had to be removed. In the early days, locomotives burnt coke as their fuel, and there must have been cases of carbon monoxide poisoning, due to inadequate ventilation. W. Adams' first outside cylinder 4-4-0s, built at Stratford in 1876 for the GER, were ungainly looking machines, but when Adams assumed control at Nine Elms in 1878, he was influenced by the graceful lines of his predecessor's locomotives which, in turn, had been influenced by the firm of Beyer Peacock of Manchester. He quickly found that, on the LSWR, his original design of 4-4-0 tank did not carry enough coal and water, so he altered it to a 4-4-2 tank by adding a bunker. More were built and one of them, very graceful 4-4-2 tank No. 488, built in 1885, has been preserved in working order on the Bluebell Railway.

Plate 32: LMS 4-4-2T No. 2090 is pictured outside Upminster Shed. The design of this locomotive subsequently developed into that of the standard LT&S 4-4-2 tanks, of which *Thundersley* is preserved at Bressingham, and examples of which were built by the LMS. The small Tilbury 4-4-2 tanks, dating from 1880, are believed to have been designed by W. Adams.

In 1883 Beyer Peacock built the first of a series of outside cylinder 4-4-0s for the Lynn & Fakenham Railway, which lasted until the 1930s on the Midland & Great Northern Railway. They closely resembled those being built by Adams at Nine Elms at the same time.

In 1903, the Norfolk & Suffolk Joint Committee opened the line from Yarmouth Beach to Lowestoft. To work this line, in 1904, the M&GN built a 4-4-2 tank locomotive using some spare parts from the Beyer Peacock 4-4-0s of 1883. Two more followed, one in 1909, and another in 1910. When comparison of *Plates 32* and *33* is made, it will be seen that there is a striking resemblance between the LT&S and M&GN 4-4-2 tank engines, and that both bear a resemblance to W. Adams' 4-4-2 tank No. 488.

Plate 33: M&GN 4-4-2T No. 20, is seen on a Cromer Beach to Yarmouth Beach train, near Mundesley.

Plate 36 (below): SR 'Schools' class 3-cylinder 4-4-0, No. 918 *Hurstpierpoint*, working an 'up' train in 1934, is seen leaving Tonbridge. At this time, the 'Lord Nelsons' were making heavy weather of the climb up to Sevenoaks on the Continental boat trains, and the easing of the Tonbridge curve gave them a better start up the bank. A contractor's Peckett 0-6-0T locomotive can be seen in the sidings.

Plate 34 (top left): During World War I, fifty Adams 0-6-0s were sent to the Middle East, with the result that some of the older LSWR locomotives lasted a very long time, in order to make good their loss. Here we see Adams Southern Railway 7ft. 1in. Class X2 4-4-0 No. 592 on a freight train near Brockenhurst. With its 7ft. 1in. driving wheels, its progress was slow and majestic.

Plate 35: A most unusual view of an SR Adams 6ft. 7in. Class X6 4-4-0, No. 658, built in 1895, and rebuilt with a Drummond type boiler, piloting Southern Railway Adams 7ft. 1in. Class X2 4-4-0 No. 590, built in 1891, climbing up from Andover Junction. There was tremendous room for the development of the 4-4-0 class and this reached its zenith in the Southern Railway 3-cylinder 'Schools', first built in 1930.

W. Adams resigned in 1895 and was succeeded at Nine Elms by Dugald Drummond. Drummond, Stroudley and Samuel Johnson had all been together for a short time in the early 1860s at Cowlairs, where they must have thrashed out every aspect of locomotive design. In 1865, Stroudley took Drummond with him to the Highland Railway at Inverness, and then in 1869 to Brighton as his Works Manager.

Drummond returned to Cowlairs in 1875 as Chief Mechanical Engineer, and in 1878 built his first inside cylinder 4-4-0 locomotive. In 1882, he moved to the Caledonian Railway at St. Rollox, where he built his first Caledonian 4-4-0, in 1884. In 1885, R. W. Urie became his chief draughtsman.

Drummond resigned from St. Rollox in 1890, where in 1895, R. W. Urie became Works Manager under J. F. McIntosh, and it is said that it was at Urie's suggestion that a large boiler was fitted to the 'Dunalastair' class 4-4-0s making them, at that time, the foremost 4-4-0s in the country. In 1897, R. W. Urie once again joined Drummond, this time at Nine Elms.

Plate 37 (above): Drummond's first 4-4-0 design for the LSWR — SR Class C8 4-4-0 No. 293, built in 1898, is seen on a freight train at Andover Town. Only ten of these locomotives were built. The next series, the T9s, built in 1899, had a larger firebox and a 10ft. coupled wheelbase. The C8 class was never altered and its boiler became standard for his 0-4-4 tanks and the K10 4-4-0s.

Plate 38 (top right): The larger fireboxes fitted to the sixty five T9s greatly improved the steaming of the locomotives. The first T9 to be rebuilt with a superheater was in 1922, and, by 1929, all the class had been so treated. These sixty five locomotives proved to be excellent machines. They retained their slide valves, which were given improved lubrication. In this view, SR Class T9 No. 280 is seen entering Bere Alston with a Plymouth to Exeter local train. The Callington branch can be seen coming in on the right. On a clear day, a trip on the branch was an unforgettable experience with its breathtaking views over Dartmoor. It was opened in 1908 by the Plymouth, Devonport & South Western Junction Railway, and was incorporated into the Southern Railway in 1923. It possessed two Hawthorn Leslie 0-6-2 tanks and one small Hawthorn Leslie 0-6-0T.

Plate 39 (right): An ex-PD&SW Junction Railway Hawthorn Leslie SR 0-6-2T, No. 757, *Earl of Mount Edgcumbe*, is being coaled at Callington — not an easy operation due to the very small bunker. The coaches are interesting having been converted from the short-lived steam railmotor cars.

Plate 40: SR Class T9 No. 733, with a mixed train, approaches Padstow. A journey on a mixed train was always exciting, as there was the possibility of some rope shunting in a wayside goods yard. I can remember a journey on a mixed train over the Helston branch, on the GWR, where the truck next to the passenger coach had lost a buffer. It was most interesting to lean out of the window and watch it take the curves.

Plate 42 (opposite): The gradient down to Dorking Tunnel is portrayed. SR Class L12 4-4-0 No. 422, basically a standard Drummond Class T9 fitted with a larger boiler and larger cylinders, is hauling a Victoria to Bognor express. Box Hill is seen in the background. The tare weight of this train, composed of modern Maunsell corridor stock, with a Pullman car, weighed 292 tons (empty), yet only 12 years earlier, there were still some set trains of Stroudley 4-wheeled coaches in daily use. These coaches could seat 50 passengers with a tare weight of under 7 tons (they resembled the coach shown in *Plate 2*). I can remember travelling in one of these, dated Brighton Works 1877. We suddenly heard heavy footsteps on the roof (rather frightening) — a trap door opened and an oil lamp was inserted. The partitions were only carried half-way up to the roof, so two lamps lit the whole coach. Just outside the carriage window a lady was demanding a foot warmer from the porter, which, as she was travelling first class, she was given. When we asked for one too, all we got was a very rude reply. Two or three of the most decrepit of these set trains of 14 coaches had 'not to be used beyond Coulsdon or Holmwood' painted on the underframe. One never to be forgotten day, my brother and I found one of these trains at Holmwood. We left late behind a Class E3 4ft. 6in. 0-6-2 tank, and our descent down the bank to Dorking must have surpassed that of Queen Victoria's funeral train. The Stroudley sets did not survive long into the 1920s, although some lasted several years longer on the Isle of Wight. Stroudley's set trains were made up either in 7 or 14 coach formations. During off peak periods, the suburban trains would only be composed of a 7 coach set. Rigid economy had always been the policy of the LB&SR since, in the 1860s, it had only just escaped bankruptcy due to the financial genius of Samuel Laing.

Plate 41: A Class T9 fitted with a 6-wheeled tender, SR 4-4-0 No. 310, with a 'down' Victoria to Bognor train, leaves the tunnel at Dorking. The coach next to the locomotive is an ex-LB&SCR non-corridor balloon (as they were called). The very liberal Brighton loading gauge will be noted, as will the 'Reduce Speed' notice at the tunnel mouth. These notices were typical Brighton line practice. In 1901 Queen Victoria died at Osborne, on the Isle of Wight, and her body was brought up to London by special train which left Fareham ten minutes late. The driver was told to reach Victoria punctually, if possible, so as not to keep King Edward VII waiting. This he succeeded in doing, but not before some of the railway officials had some anxious moments. The track near the tunnel mouth at Dorking, shown in this photograph, was very spongy, and it gave the Royal passengers a rough ride at the speed at which they were travelling. There is a severe reverse curve at the other end of the tunnel. The Kaiser had evidently not been overawed by the occasion and had thoroughly enjoyed it, as, on arrival at Victoria, he sent his equerry to congratulate the driver.

In 1901, Drummond introduced a mixed traffic 4-4-0 locomotive for the LSWR, and 40 of these engines were built. They had 5ft. 7in. driving wheels and a C8 type boiler, and were known as Class K10. They were very similar to some small 4-4-0s he had designed in 1888 for the Caledonian Railway.

In 1903, he built another 40 similar locomotives, Class L11. These had the standard T9 boiler with longer fireboxes. Unlike the T9s, no Class K10 or L11 4-4-0 was ever superheated.

Plate 43: SR Class L11 5ft. 7in. 4-4-0 No. 410, piloting Class T9 6ft. 7in. 4-4-0 No. 721, is pictured on a sightseeing excursion train at Corfe Castle. At Swanage, the 4,000 gallon tenders had to be emptied of water before it was possible to turn the locomotives. The train had been worked down to Bournemouth by a 'King Arthur' class locomotive, then hauled to Swanage, and back to Salisbury by the two 4-4-0s, and returned to Waterloo behind a 'Lord Nelson'. It ran slow through the New Forest and down the Swanage branch, so that the passengers could admire the countryside.

Plate 44 (top right): So far, this book has been largely dominated by the locomotives of three men, Samuel Johnson, William Stroudley and Dugald Drummond. There were many other designers, and here we have a 6ft. 9in. Class D7 4-4-0 No. 5684, built by Thomas Parker in 1891, to an 1887 design, for the Manchester, Sheffield & Lincolnshire Railway, which subsequently became part of the Great Central Railway. The photograph was taken at Cleethorpes and shows No. 5684 about to leave on a New Holland train composed of old 6-wheeled coaches.

Plate 45 (right): A Manchester to Liverpool express passes Glazebrook with LNER 7ft. Class D6 4-4-0 No. 5876 in charge. This locomotive was built in 1898 for the London extension of the MS&L Railway to London. On this service, they were very soon replaced by the larger-boilered Class D9 4-4-0s, and spent most of their lives working on the lines of the Cheshire Lines Committee.

Plate 46: LNER Class D10 No. 5430 *Purdon Viccars* is seen on an 'up' slow working near Amersham. One of this class, GCR No. 506 *Butler Henderson* is now preserved in working order at Loughborough.

The large boilered 4-4-0 'Dunalastair' class, introduced in 1896 on the Caledonian Railway, was copied by nearly every railway company in the country. For the first time the driver had a reliable supply of steam, but loads were steadily increasing, and it was clear that the only way the 4-4-0 locomotive could be enlarged was by the employment of an extra axle. So in 1898, therefore, H. Ivatt, who had succeeded Patrick Stirling at Doncaster in 1896, introduced the first 4-4-2 in this country. The extra axle was not coupled. The class, following American practice, were called Atlantics. In 1902 Ivatt increased the size of their boilers only to find the locomotive was not as successful as he had hoped.

What he had now got was a boiler full of wet steam, with a corresponding increase in coal and water consumption. When his successor, Sir Nigel Gresley, later rebuilt the Atlantics with superheaters and new cylinders fitted with piston valves, their performance was revolutionised. On the East Coast route to Scotland, both Darlington and the NBR at Cowlairs built Atlantics for their expresses. On the L&Y at Horwich, Sir J. Aspinall had built an inside cylinder 4-4-2 in 1899, and had provided a few of them with a very primitive form of superheater, or steam drier.

Plate 47 (top right): An LNER Class C1 4-4-2, No. 4411, hauls an 'up' Cambridge buffet car express near Royston. These trains were very sharply timed and were very popular. With their small cylinders, the Atlantics always put up a rousing performance on the hilly parts of the journey. D. Earle Marsh had been appointed Chief Assistant Mechanical Engineer at Doncaster in 1895, and prior to this, he had been Assistant Works Manager at Swindon. He was appointed Locomotive Superintendent at Brighton in 1905 on the death of R. J. Billinton, and his first locomotives (built in 1905 by Kitson & Co., Leeds) were almost identical to H. Ivatt's Class C1 4-4-2s of 1902.

Plate 48 (right): An SR Class H1 Marsh 4-4-2 No. 2038 *Portland Bill* passes Rodmell & Southease on an 'up' Newhaven boat train.

Plate 49: An SR Class H1 Marsh 4-4-2, No. 2039 *Hartland Point* heads a 'down' military special near Gatwick. The locomotive had been cut down to the standard Southern Railway loading gauge. After the Grouping, H1s were fitted with superheaters.

Plate 50: SR Class H2 No. 20422 *North Foreland*, pilots SR Class B1 4-4-0 No. 1445, on an 'up' Newhaven boat train near Rodmell & Southease. No. 2422 had not yet been cut down to the standard Southern Railway loading gauge. The Class H2 series of 4-4-2s were built, in 1911, with large cylinders and superheaters. They were very quiet runners when compared with the small cylinder H1s. Both classes gave excellent service and lasted well into British Railways' days, when they could haul trains of up to 450 tons, unpiloted. Southern Railway locomotive No. 1445, the train engine, was built at Ashford in 1898 to a design of James Stirling. The Class B 4-4-0 had a slightly larger boiler than the Class F locomotive, but the larger boilers made no difference to their performance, and all except two of the class were rebuilt with the standard F1 boiler.

The first 4-6-0 locomotive in the British Isles was built for the Highland Railway in 1894 by Sharp Stewart. It never seems to have been satisfactorily explained how this important development took place on a small Scottish line.

During World War II, almost identical locomotives (but built to the South African Railways' 3ft. 6in. gauge) were shunting on the quay at Cape Town. Did David Jones, who succeeded Stroudley as Chief Mechanical Engineer of the Highland Railway in 1869, and who retired in 1896, actually design these 4-6-0s, or did he adapt a Sharp Stewart proven Colonial design? What a fascinating story there must be waiting to be written about British Colonial locomotives.

The GWR built their first 4-6-0 locomotive in 1896, and carried out continuous research until 1906. A prototype 2-cylinder 4-6-0 appeared in 1902, and then, in 1903, the GWR purchased a 4-cylinder De Glehn Compound 4-4-2 locomotive from France, and followed it with two more in 1905.

In 1906 appeared the first modern GWR 4-cylinder 4-6-0 locomotive, No. 40 *North Star*. This engine was built as a 4-4-2 and was not altered to a 4-6-0 until 1909. This continuous ten years of research put Swindon about 25 years ahead of any of its contemporaries.

In 1922, the GNR built the first of Gresley's 4-6-2 locomotives — No. 1470 *Great Northern*. This engine, as built, could be called one of the last of the old-fashioned British express locomotives.

In 1923, the GWR built the first of the 'Castle' class 4-6-0s (the logical development of *North Star*). In 1925, after the locomotive exchange between a 'Castle' and one of Sir Nigel Gresley's original Pacifics, the latter were fitted with all modern modifications. In consequence, with the introducion in the mid-1930s of the high speed East Coast and West Coast expresses, steam may be said to have reached its finest hour.

Plate 51: A GWR 4-cylinder 4-6-0, No. 5059 *Powis Castle* heads the 'up' night mail near Marazion (6.45p.m. ex-Penzance). When this photograph was taken in 1937, on three nights a week the locomotive on the 'up' train was booked to work through to Paddington via Bristol — 325 miles. The mail bags could be picked up or dropped at speed on this train. This was the first *Powis Castle* which ran as such for only five months. During the previous year, Swindon had constructed some small 4-4-0s, using parts from the existing 'Duke' and 'Bulldog' classes. Consequently they became known as 'Dukedogs', one of which is now preserved on the Bluebell Railway. The 'Dukedogs' were originally named after Earls. Their Lordships then complained to the Directors of the GWR that they did not consider such small locomotives worthy of their distinguished names, so 21 'Castle' class 4-6-0s were then renamed after the 'complaining' Earls. No. 5059 was one of these, being renamed *Earl St. Aldwyn*. In 1939, one of the new batch of 'Castles', No. 5082, was once more named *Powis Castle* but in 1940, in a moment of patriotism, twelve 'Castles' were renamed after aircraft which had distinguished themselves in the 'Battle of Britain', and the second *Powis Castle* was one of these, and for the second time lost its original name. In 1949 another batch of 'Castles' was built, and No. 7024 became the third and last *Powis Castle*.

The 'Castles' of 1923 developed into the 'Kings' of 1927, and Swindon steam supremacy reigned unchallenged until about 1935. After Gresley's Pacifics had been modernised, there was a tremendous resurgence of locomotive development. For sheer enjoyment of locomotive performance there was nothing to beat a journey on the 'down' 'Cornish Riviera Express'; the 10.30a.m. Paddington to Plymouth — 225 miles non-stop in 240 minutes. By a judicious discussion on scarlet fever, it was sometimes possible, even on a very full train, to get an empty compartment next to the locomotive. Then with both windows wide open, one could rush freely from side to side and log the journey unimpeded in any way. There was always an exciting expectancy about travel on this train, especially when one left Paddington with a load that entitled the driver to stop and take on a pilot from Newton Abbot. To do this he liked to have at least five minutes in hand for the stop at Newton Abbot, to take on the pilot locomotive for the Dainton and Rattery inclines. On one occasion with a heavy train, which was going to be over the unpiloted limit, we ran into trouble immediately on leaving Paddington. Without any signal checks or permanent way slowings, we were ten minutes late by Westbury. Time was then regained steadily, but the locomotive was clearly winded again by the climb to Whiteball. We were still five minutes late through Exeter, and then the question arose — what would the driver do at Newton Abbot? More fast running followed, until steam was shut off for the long gentle curve round to the station. The weather was fine, the distant signal was off. We ran quietly and slowly down the platform, and still there was no sign of what was going to happen. Then suddenly, in the centre of the station, without any warning, all hell was let loose — the driver was going to try and make a punctual arrival at Plymouth by not stopping to take on the pilot to which he was entitled. Never before or since have I heard any locomotive make such a glorious noise. We accelerated hard to Aller Junction and then speed began falling as we tackled Dainton Bank. The blast from the locomotive reverberated from side to side of the rocky cutting, but we topped the summit successfully and No. 6026 *King John* had cleared his biggest hurdle. Then followed a magnificently controlled descent to Totnes, followed by the further climb up to Rattery. Once over this summit, there was a rather faster than usual descent to Plymouth, touching 72m.p.h. down Hemerdon Bank, and we finally stopped at Plymouth 10 seconds late. The driver and fireman were completely black from head to toe. There was just time for the driver to smile and say 'We had terrible coal the whole way down, but I have a wonderful mate'.

Coming back after the holiday I had an unexpected trip on the footplate of No. 6015 *King Richard III* from Exeter to Taunton. We were held up at Burlescombe for four minutes by the signal, but we started on the gradient without any trouble, and finally swept down Wellington Bank, not at 100m.p.h., but it seemed very close to it. That evening I heard for the first time a piece of music that became very popular in the 1930s — Pacific 2-3-1 by Arthur Honegger. I would advise anyone who wants to know what a footplate trip on a 'King' sounds like to get this record, if it is still possible, and to play it turn and turn about with one of Peter Handford's tapes.

During the 1930s, the GWR ran a prestige train, chiefly for the benefit of railway officials returning from Swindon to London. To begin with it was a light train of 5, 6, or 7 bogies, leaving Swindon at 3.45p.m. and completing the journey in 65 minutes. To fill the train, a special 5s. 0d. (today's value 25p) ticket was issued, which allowed one to go down the line on the 12.45p.m. ex-Paddington train, getting to Swindon about 2.30p.m., in time to take the 3.45p.m. back. This was a delightful train. I remember on one occasion when we were going along by the river near Pangbourne, the 'Oxford eight' were practising for the boat race in beautiful spring sunshine. It seemed from the train as if they were beating us — they beat Cambridge that year.

The GWR was always a line of many contrasts. On one such 25p visit to Swindon there was suddenly a stamp of feet, and a heavy hand fell on my shoulder. It was a policeman demanding my roll of film. I still wonder to this day what dreadful thing I had unwittingly photographed.

Plate 52: This shows the prestige train, referred to, near Cheltenham, hauled by a small 2-6-2 tank. It reversed at Gloucester where the London-bound 'Castle' backed on. The coaches all carried headboards 'Cheltenham Flyer'; later it became known as the 'Swindon Flyer'.

Dugald Drummond, having spent roughly seven years at Cowlairs, seven at St. Rollox, seven in private business, seven at Nine Elms, was, in 1903, again beginning to get restless. In 1905, he applied for a similar job at Brighton on the death of R. J. Billinton, but the Brighton Directors would have none of him, so he turned his mind, at the age of 65, to building a 4-cylinder 4-6-0 locomotive, which the increased weight of the trains had shown to be necessary. It had taken the GWR about ten years of continuous research to achieve success with this type, so it is not surprising that his 4-6-0s were mostly failures.

Plate 53: This photograph shows the most successful of Drummond's 4-6-0s, the Class T14 4-cylinder type. No. 447 is pictured on a 'down' slow Waterloo to Portsmouth train, near Guildford. The North Downs can be seen in the background, and on the right are the remains of the loop that once ran round to the Guildford to Redhill line. No. 447 is a 'dinosaur' of a locomotive, with a wonderful sweep from the boiler over the outside cylinders. Its mammoth tender, carrying 5,800 gallons of water, would indicate its heavy water consumption — not to be wondered at when one considers the terrific wall of air it had to push before it.

Plate 54: SR Class 415 6ft. No. 332. R. W. Urie, who had followed Drummond from St. Rollox, succeeded him at Eastleigh in 1912, and then did what he could to improve Drummond's 4-6-0s, which was very little. No. 332 was a 2-cylinder rebuild of a 6ft. 4-cylinder locomotive, but in point of fact only the very massive boiler shell was used again. In spite of its very high pitch, the boiler on No. 447 was not as large. No. 332 was very solidly built, like all Urie's locomotives, and performed a great deal of heavy unspectacular work. There are several records of them touching speeds of over 80m.p.h., especially with Salisbury drivers.

Plate 55 (left): SR 4-6-0 No. 736 *Excalibur* was built at Eastleigh in 1918. This was Urie's first passenger 4-6-0 locomotive and it is shown near Winchester Junction on a Bournemouth to Oxford Sunday excursion. It was the prototype of the well-known 'King Arthur' class. Twenty of Urie's 4-6-0s were built by the LSWR. After the 1923 Grouping, Maunsell built a further series employing the well-tried GWR principles. These proved very successful and No. 777 *Sir Lamiel*, of this class, is preserved in working order at the National Railway Museum, York.

Plate 56 (bottom left): SR mixed traffic 4-6-0 No. 474, built to Urie's design in 1924, heads an 'up' boat special and is seen leaving Southampton Docks. The photograph shows a delightful mixture of locomotive, Pullman cars, lorries and bicycles.

Plate 57: In 1926, Maunsell produced his 4-cylinder 4-6-0 'Lord Nelson' class, but in spite of it having a modern front-end layout, its performance proved disappointing, probably largely due to defects in the design of its grate. In this view, SR 4-cylinder 4-6-0 No. 857 *Lord Howe* hauls the 'down' 'Atlantic Coast Express' near Andover. It had recently been fitted with a new boiler having a combustion chamber, as part of an experiment to try to find a locomotive that could keep time with the heaviest Continental boat trains between Victoria and Dover. At this time, the bulk of the Continental traffic still travelled by rail. A heavy train of sleeping cars which ran through from London to Paris had just been introduced. *Lord Howe's* boiler must have had the smallest dome ever built, but its boiler showed no improvement and had a very short life. Maunsell was succeeded in 1937 by Oliver Bulleid, who had been Sir Nigel Gresley's second in command at Doncaster. He immediately set about improving the 'Lord Nelsons', and by modifying their front ends and their grates, vastly improved their performance. One could always tell, in the blackout during the war years, if a 'Lord Nelson' was at the head of the train by the way it would get away without any difficulty with a very heavy load from stations like Surbiton and Woking. There were only sixteen in the class and they were very quickly overshadowed by Bulleids Pacifics, but they performed excellent work after modification.

Plate 58: An SR Class N15X 4-6-0, No. 2332 *Stroudley*, heads a 'down' slow working near Basingstoke. The track had been relaid overnight, hence the cloud of dust. Seven of these locomotives had originally been built at Brighton — the first in 1914, as 4-6-4 tanks. They were converted at Eastleigh to 4-6-0s after the Brighton and Eastbourne electrification had left them with no more suitable work. During World War II six were transferred on loan to the Great Western Railway. In his book *Firing Days — Reminiscences of a Great Western Fireman*, Mr H. Gasson praises them highly.

Plate 59: In 1903, J. G. Robinson, Chief Mechanical Engineer of the Great Central Railway, built two almost identical 4-4-2s and 4-6-0s. The 4-4-2s proved most successful and worked the Leicester to Marylebone express trains for the next thirty years, despite the introduction of more modern types. The 4-6-0s were used on a greater variety of traffic, especially the fast fish trains. A further ten were built in 1906. This view shows one of these engines, LNER Class B4 6ft. 7in. 4-6-0 No. 6104, leaving Lincoln with a 'down' express. It carries the passenger green livery.

Plate 60: One of Robinson's 4-cylinder 5ft. 7in. mixed traffic 4-6-0s, pictured near Glazebrook on the Cheshire Lines Committee system, with a train from Liverpool Docks. These locomotives were very powerful. There were also six similar passenger locomotives with 6ft. 9in. driving wheels. These were used for two or three years on the 'Yorkshire Pullman' trains from King's Cross, but the drivers seem to have preferred their Great Northern Atlantics which, at the time, were performing at the height of their power. Of the two other constituents of the East Coast Main Line, the NER at Darlington first tried 4-6-0s but finally, like Robinson on the GCR, preferred Atlantics for express work. The NBR at Cowlairs used Atlantics, based largely on Robinson's Great Central design.

Locomotive development on the LNWR had been different from the other lines. In 1882, Francis Webb, the autocratic Chief Mechanical Engineer, produced his first Compounds, various classes of which were built for the next twenty one years. These Compounds seem to have been more controversial than the Bulleid Pacifics of the Southern Railway. Webb was succeeded in 1903 by George Whale who immediately started to withdraw them and build afresh. There is thus no photograph of a Webb Compound in this book, as I should have liked.

Plate 61: This shows one of George Whale's 'Precursor' class 4-4-0s, which makes an interesting comparison with the renewed 'Jumbo' shown in *Plate 3*. LMS No. 5271 *Gaelic*, on a Bletchley train, is pictured leaving Cambridge. The first 'Precursor' class locomotive was built in 1904.

In 1905, Whale had built the 'Experiment' class 4-6-0s with 6ft. 3in. driving wheels for the harder northern section of the LNWR main line from Crewe to Carlisle. Like so many other 4-6-0s, with a shallower longer firebox than a 'Precursor' 4-4-0, they were never really popular. Curiously, they had a very good turn of speed, for their 6ft. 3in. driving wheels.

Plate 64 (below): As the superheated 'George V' class 4-4-0s followed the 'Precursors', so the 'Prince of Wales' class 4-6-0s followed the 'Experiments'. This view shows LMS 'Prince of Wales' class superheated 4-6-0 No. 5777 with the 'down' relief 'Irish Mail' express, picking up water from the troughs at Prestatyn.

Plate 62 (top left): LMS 4-4-0 No. 5243 *Lapwing*, a 'Precursor' class locomotive rebuilt with superheater, new cylinders and extended smokebox. It is seen, most unusually, working a 'down' Birmingham 2 hour express near Bletchley. I was fortunate to capture this scene as late as 1933. When the LMS first introduced Midland type 4-4-0 Compounds on the Birmingham trains in 1925, there was considerable opposition, some of the older drivers still having memories of Webb's Compounds.

Plate 63 (left): The 'George V' class superheated 4-4-0s followed the 'Precursors', and this view shows LMS 'George V' class 4-4-0 No. 5386 *Edward Tootal* passing Canonbury, with a meat train from London Docks.

In 1908, Whale retired to be succeeded in 1909 by C. J. Bowen-Cooke. In five years, Whale had completely put the LNWR back on its feet. In 1913, C. J. Bowen-Cooke produced a 4-cylinder 4-6-0, the first of which was named *Sir Gilbert Claughton*. A final series of these was built as late as 1920. Their fireboxes, like those of the 'Experiments', seem to have been hard to fire.

Plate 65: LMS superheated 'Precursor' class 4-4-0 No. 5303 *Argus* pilots LMS 4-cylinder 'Claughton' class 4-6-0 No. 5937 with an 'up' express near Blisworth. It seems that *Argus* was the nom de plume of one of Webb's bitterest critics in the technical press. He retaliated by naming one of his 'Dreadnought' class Compounds after him.

Plate 66: An LMS 4-cylinder 'Claughton' class 4-6-0 No. 5913 *Colonel Lockwood* hauls the 'down' 14 coach 'Mancunian' near Bletchley in 1933. The maximum unpiloted load laid down for a 'Claughton' on an express from Euston to Crewe was 420 tons. *Colonel Lockwood* must have been hauling a total load of about 500 tons.

Plate 67: LMS 4-cylinder 4-6-0 No. 5991 *C. H. Bowen-Cooke* heads an 'up' express near Tring. Weight restrictions limited the size of the boilers on these 'Claughtons'. The photographs in this section of the book, taken in 1933, show the 'Claughtons' still taking a full share of the main line express work, yet large scale withdrawals began in the same year and continued throughout 1934. Sir William Stanier's new LMS standard 4-6-0s completely took over all the main line services.

Plate 68: This shows the final Crewe 4-cylinder 4-6-0 development — the 1928 rebuilding of twenty 'Claughtons' with large boileers. Ten of these were fitted with Caprotti valve gear. Shown here is LMS reboilered Caprotti 4-cylinder 4-6-0 No. 6023 *Sir Charles Cust* with an 'up' express, near Abergele. These rebuilds had a short life. Their boilers were standard with those of the first forty 3-cylinder 4-6-0 'Baby Scots'.

Plate 69: The new LMS era is illustrated here by a photograph of 'Royal Scot' class 3-cylinder 4-6-0 locomotive No. 6126 *Sanspareil* with a 15 coach 'down' express near Tring.

Plate 70: 'Royal Scot' class 3-cylinder 4-6-0 locomotive, No. 6111 *Royal Fusilier*, heads an 'up' Aberdeen fish train, near Gleneagles.

Plate 71: An LMS 3-cylinder 'Jubilee' class 4-6-0, No. 5573 *Newfoundland* passes Minshull Vernon with an 'up' express. This locomotive has a small standard tender and top feed on the boiler.

Plate 72: An LMS 3-cylinder 'Royal Scot' class 4-6-0. No. 6136 *The Border Regiment* heads an 'up' express, and passes 3-cylinder 4-6-0 'Jubilee' No. 5629 *Straits Settlements* at Minshull Vernon. No. 5629 has a high-sided tender and top feed on the dome.

Plate 75 (below):   LMS Class 3 0-6-0 No. 3768 was a member of the class which had been rebuilt from a Class 2, being fitted with a larger boiler in a similar manner to the small 4-4-0s. No. 3768 is seen approaching Towcester on an Easter Monday race special from St. Pancras. This was a once a year train, and was the only passenger train to use the freight only line from Ravenswood Junction, on the Bedford to Northampton branch, to Towcester. This route was largely used by banana trains from Bristol Docks to St. Pancras, running mostly by night. The train is composed of eight Midland clerestory coaches. Locomotives were changed at Bedford. The previous year, a standard LMS Class 4 0-6-0 had been used, but it had proved impossible to turn the locomotive until all the water had been emptied from the tender.

Plate 73 (top left):   Class 5 4-6-0 No. 5031 at Berkeley Road, which was the first 'Black Five' I had seen. It had been shunted to allow the passage of the 'down' 'Devonian'. Little did I think, when I photographed this peaceful scene, how well I would get to know the 'Black Fives' during the war.

Plate 74 (left):   From very early days, the 0-6-0 became the standard class of freight locomotive, often having a boiler standard with a passenger 2-4-0 or 4-4-0 locomotive. This view shows a typical Johnson 0-6-0 LMS Class 2 locomotive No. 3551. It is standing at Towcester on the Stratford-on-Avon & Midland Junction Railway after hauling an Easter Monday race special. Behind it is an ex-LNWR 'Cauliflower' 0-6-0. S. W. Johnson first designed an 0-6-0 at Stratford (London) in 1870 for the GER. They were smaller but very similar to No. 3551 and, in contrast to those on the Midland Railway, had a short life. Most 0-6-0s were mixed traffic locomotives and were required to be free running, in order to work excursion trains.

Plate 78 (below): I think much of the fascination of steam locomotives was due to the fact that, like people, the most unlikely ones can sometimes rise to unexpected heights. As many Johnson Class 2 0-6-0s were rebuilt with larger boilers to become Class 3, so many of R. J. Billinton's very similar small Class C2 0-6-0s were rebuilt at Brighton with a larger boiler to become Class C2X. This view shows SR Class C2X 0-6-0 No. 2550 on a Brighton to Aldershot Tattoo special Pullman train, leaving Rudgwick on the Horsham to Guildford branch. It was faced with a start up a 1 in 60 gradient with a load of 324 tons (empty). A Pullman car on this rural branch was a rarity. No. 2550 was moving at walking pace and I walked up quite a long way, pushing on the rear buffer.

Plate 76 (top left): This shows the final development of the Johnson 0-6-0 LMS Class 4. No. 4414 is pictured on a Leicester train entering Bourne on the M&GN. The old GNR cast-iron urinal, dating from 1858, will be noted on the platform. One of these is now preserved on the East Somerset Railway at Cranmore.

Plate 77 (left): When R. J. Billinton came from Derby to Brighton as Chief Mechanical Engineer, following the death of William Stroudley, the second type of locomotive he designed was an 0-6-0 (the first being an 0-4-4 tank). The family likeness to the Derby locomotives can be seen, although the original boiler, with spring balances on the dome, had been replaced. The train is shown at Bognor, the locomotive being SR Class C2 0-6-0 No. B533. This photograph reminds me of the happiest man I have ever met. It was the day before my final medical examination, and I had decided to take a walk on the South Downs to clear my head. Returning home from Lewes behind Class L ex-SECR 4-4-0 No. 1764, the locomotive began to falter and then stopped, seemingly miles from anywhere. The fireman said they had burst a tube. After about twenty minutes, No. 1764 had sufficient steam to restart and slowly made its way to Hayward's Heath. Here, SR Class E5 0-6-2T No. 2404 piloted us to Three Bridges. After about ten minutes, the Three Bridges yard pilot, Class C2 0-6-0 No. B555, came slowly down from the shed, As she passed us the driver's face was lit by a shaft of light, and a passenger commented on the fact that he had never before seen such a happy-looking man. No. B555 backed on to the train, and then there followed a superb piece of driving from Three Bridges to East Croydon — something I shall never forget. I had to alight at East Croydon and spoke to the driver who said, 'I am the happiest man in the country. I retire in two days time and my one ambition was to have a final trip up the main line, which I have achieved this evening'. He said that when they left Three Bridges, No. 1764 was just about pulling herself and her tender, but from Earlswood, she had only been pulling herself. It was a clear night and I watched No. B555 proudly leaving East Croydon with all her signals winking green and with No. 1764 in tow. The skill of a lifetime had been packed into the last half hour. At next day's examinations, when I went up to the invigilator to hear the result, he shook me by the hand and said 'Congratulations Dr. Allen' — and I was then the second happiest man in the country.

Plate 79: East Kent Railway 0-6-0 No. 6 hauls a mixed train, near Wingham. This locomotive, formerly an SECR 0-6-0 Class O, had been obtained from the Southern Railway in 1923. It had been built in 1891 to an 1878 design which James Stirling had first used for the G&SWR. The typical Stirling cab and domeless boiler should be noted.

Plate 80: SR Class C 0-6-0 No. A223 heads a Gravesend West to Swanley Junction train and is seen passing Fawkham Junction. The coaches are an ex-LBSC motor-train set. The Class C locomotives were strongly built and, in design, owed more to Longhedge than to Ashford. They had a good turn of speed when used on passenger services.

Plate 81: An LMS 'Cauliflower' 5ft. 0-6-0, No. 8521, pilots a standard 2-6-2T at Blaenau Festiniog. These 0-6-0s were frequently used on passenger trains.

Plate 82: LMS 0-6-0 No. 2884 carries out shunting duties on the Somerset & Dorset Railway. The driver was a great authority on the Arthurian legend, and we spent a very happy morning on the footplate shunting up and down hearing all about King Arthur and his Knights of the Round Table. No. 2884 was designed by S. W. Johnson in 1878 for the S&DJR. It was smaller than his standard class, having 4ft. 6in. driving wheels.

Plate 83: For heavy coal traffic, the 0-6-0 developed into the 0-8-0, of which a great many were built, especially by the Northern lines. This scene shows LMS ex-LNWR 0-8-0 No. 9439, near Tring, on a very long train of empty coal trucks returning north. At this time, most wagons were privately-owned, and required special marshalling.

Plate 84: The 0-8-0s were not often used on passenger services and this view shows No. 9439 hauling a special train near Thelwall on the Liverpool to Manchester line, via Warrington.

Plate 85: In turn, the 0-8-0 type developed into the 2-8-0 and this view shows LNER 2-8-0 No. 6315 with a coal train, passing Brocklesby. Originally built for the GCR at Gorton Works, the type was taken as a War Office standard in World War I and many were sent to the Middle East in both world wars. It was very reassuring to see this class and the standard LMS 2-8-0s working in Egypt, when one had been a long time out of England.

The 2-6-0 was a surprisingly long time developing, probably because of the difficulty in designing a satisfactory pony truck. The first example was built in 1878 by William Adams for the GER and had 'MOGUL' painted on its large sand box; a generic name which stuck to the type as long as steam locomotives existed. This class had an exceedingly short life of about six to seven years.

At the turn of the century, Parliamentary legislation limited the number of hours that could be worked by footplate crews, resulting in a sudden demand for more locomotives. The Midland Railway and Great Northern Railway met the demand by importing small 2-6-0s from America. They too had a very short life.

Plate 86: In 1901, the GWR built an outside-framed 2-6-0 for freight work, and then in 1911 came the first of a long series of mixed traffic 5ft. 8in. Moguls. This photograph shows one of these locomotives, GWR 2-6-0 No. 6301, working a Redhill to Reading train, near Deepdene, on the Southern Railway. It was rare for a locomotive of one company to be rostered regularly over another company's line. The scene was captured in 1938 when it was clear that another major war was imminent, and that the Redhill to Reading line might have, once again, a great part to play in it, requiring Great Western drivers at Reading to have knowledge of the route. In the event, the line bore the brunt of the evacuation from Dunkirk in 1940. The only fact that the Prince Consort got wrong, when he used his influence to get the line built for military reasons in the 1840s was that, in 1940, it was the French who were our allies and not our enemies, as he had expected.

Plate 87: In 1913, L. Billinton, who had succeeded Marsh at Brighton, built the first of seventeen successful 2-6-0s. This view shows one of these locomotives, SR Class K 2-6-0 No. B353, fitted with a top feed boiler and working a 'down' Worthing express composed of of ex-LC&D six wheelers. These coaches were fitted with wooden slatted seats and were latterly used mainly for hop-pickers' specials.

In 1913, Maunsell became Chief Mechanical Engineer and asked several Swindon trained men to join his team at Ashford. The result was that in 1917, there appeared the first SECR 5ft. 6in. 2-6-0. This was an historic design, as it was the first locomotive outside Swindon to have long travel valve gear and streamlined steam passages — the secret of successful locomotives which Churchward had discovered after long research, a dozen years earlier.

Plate 88 (above): SR Class N 5ft. 6in. 2-6-0 No. 1812 heads an 'up' Bognor to Victoria train near Ford Junction. The stock is unusually interesting — an LSWR bogie van, an LBSC balloon type motor set, and an SECR three bogie set, all followed by a 4-wheeled van.

Milk traffic from Sussex to London had always hitherto been heavy, and the vans used to convey the old-fashioned milk churns were a wonderful collection of ancient vehicles.

The SECR had been impressed by the use of large tank engines on the LB&SCR, whose Class I3 4-4-2 tanks in particular were equally at home on both main line expresses and local suburban trains. They could be rostered for almost any duty, being able to run bunker first, making turning after every journey unnecessary.

In 1917, Maunsell also designed a 2-6-4T, a tank engine version of the Class N 2-6-0, but with 6ft. driving wheels. Experience soon showed that their water capacity was too low for the longer SECR runs, and that they were unsteady on tracks not in the best condition. In 1927, one rolled so badly that it became derailed, and several lives were lost in the resulting disaster at Sevenoaks. These tank locomotives, which had all been given names after rivers, were withdrawn the same evening. I can well remember this, because next day I cycled to Tadworth to photograph one of them on a regular late afternoon train, and was disappointed to find a Stirling 4-4-0, instead.

The 'River' class locomotives were all rebuilt as tender engines in 1928, but it remained possible to photograph a similar 2-cylinder 2-6-4 tank but with 5ft. 6in. driving wheels, on the Metropolitan Railway. One hundred of the SECR Class N 2-6-0s were built after World War I at Woolwich Arsenal as a relief measure, fifty of which were bought by the Southern Railway who, by waiting patiently, obtained them very cheaply in 1925. A few went to Ireland, a few to Romania, and six to the Metropolitan Railway, who altered them to 2-6-4 tank engines as shown in *Plate 89*.

The Metropolitan Railway only used the 2-6-4 tanks on passenger trains in emergencies. In the difficult post-war years they were found more frequently on such duties.

After the Sevenoaks accident, Sir Nigel Gresley carried out a series of tests on the Southern Railway's 'River' class 2-6-4 tanks. On the LNER main line near Huntingdon, he found they rode well at speeds in excess of 80m.p.h. but on the old LSWR main line, near Woking, they rolled badly.

The Southern Railway subsequently built a series of 3-cylinder 2-6-4 tanks with 5ft. 6in. driving wheels for the heavy cross-London coal trains, using the tanks off the withdrawn 'Rivers'. I never saw one of these on a passenger train.

Because of the Sevenoaks disaster, a series of 2-6-4 tanks, being planned for the Liverpool Street to Southend service, were never built by the LNER, but Sir Henry Fowler on the LMS went ahead with his 2-6-4 tanks which proved most successful, and developed into a standard BR design.

Plate 89: Metropolitan Railway 2-6-4T No. 112 hauls a freight train at Aylesbury.

Plate 90: After the Sevenoaks accident the 2-6-4 'River' class tank locomotives were rebuilt as tender locomotives. This view shows the first of the class, No. 790, built at Ashford in 1917, and rebuilt as a tender locomotive in 1928. As 6ft. Class U 2-6-0 No. 1790, it climbs Honiton Bank, in Devon, with a 'down' freight train.

Plate 91: An SR Class U 6ft. 2-6-0, No. A804, is pictured with a 13 coach through express from the Kent Coast resorts to the Midlands and Birkenhead, and the train is seen near Betchworth. This was a very heavy load for the hilly stretch of track between Reading and Guildford. During World War II, such locomotives, but with 3-cylinders instead of 2, used to work even heavier trains through from Redhill to Banbury and back.

Plate 92: An SR 2-6-0, No. 1631, which had been built new as a tender locomotive after the Sevenoaks accident, heads an 'up' freight train near Betchworth. The running plate is higher, and the driving wheel splashers are lower. It is fitted with a high capacity tender and smoke deflectors, which had proved desirable with the soft exhaust of a long travel valve gear locomotive.

Owing to lack of adhesion, the single wheeler had disappeared during the 1920s (with the exception of one or two departmental Darlington 2-2-4 tanks). It now remains to describe tank locomotives and their development.

Plate 93: SR Class D1 0-4-2T No. B629 is pictured still running with a Stroudley-type boiler. It is shown at Kensington Olympia (as it is called today) on the Clapham Junction service. This was the last regular passenger working of this class in London.

Plate 94: This shows the second of the class, SR D1M 0-4-2T No. B298, built in 1873, and it is pictured with a Brighton train at Rodwell and Southease.

Plate 95: An SR Class D1M 0-4-2T, No. B615, (Brighton 1875) heads a push and pull train leaving Ford Junction. Another Class D1 0-4-2T, No. 34, had gone new to Epsom in 1876, and in 1926 it was withdrawn from the same shed (although it had also been at other locations in the intervening years). Another Class D1 0-4-2T, No. B631, (Brighton built in 1876) had come up from Horsham in April 1933, replacing a Class I1X 4-4-2T in an emergency. Its load was four Maunsell corridors and an SECR bogie. It came into Victoria on the stroke of time, coming to rest beside one of the new Brighton electric expresses. As can be seen from the photographs, these locomotives looked surprisingly modern for their years. They were the prototype for all Drummond 0-4-4 tanks, North British, Caledonian and South Western. H. Holcroft, in his book *Locomotive Adventure*, describes four Class D1 locomotives which he found at Epsom during the General Strike of 1926 as 'my impressions of the Stroudley D1 tank were very favourable. These little engines were simple and straightforward in design and caused the minimum of trouble in doing their daily work'.

Plate 96: Unlike R. J. Billinton's designs, many of which had to be subsequently fitted with larger boilers, only two of Stroudley's locomotives ever received this treatment (and that experimentally). One was SR Class D1X No. B216, an 1875 locomotive, the other was Class E1 0-6-0T No. 689. No. B216 was stationed at West Croydon and worked turn and turn about with the Class D3 0-4-4 tanks, and Class E3 and Class E4 0-6-2 tanks — although never on freight duties. The rear trailing axle box had a tendency to run hot, so every time No. B216 came back from Brighton after a general overhaul, she was placed under the hoist and the axle box was wedged — there was never any more trouble until the next visit. Leaving the London area in June 1928, she then worked from Bognor Shed before being transferred to Eastbourne. Here she was kept in perfect condition like all other Eastbourne locomotives at that time. When the new 'Schools' class, 3-cylinder 4-4-0, No. 914 *Eastbourne* was on show for the benefit of the boys of Eastbourne College, No. B216 was on show too, beside her, and stole all the thunder. This view of No. B216 shows her near Godstone, in March 1933, on her last regular duty, from Eastbourne to Redhill, via Tonbridge, and return.

Plate 97: In *Plate 19* we saw an SR Class I1 locomotive, No. B5, with its small 4ft. 3in. boiler. This view shows LNER Class C12 4-4-2T No. 4016 at Manningtree with a Harwich train. The basic similarity between the classes can be seen.

Plate 98: SR Class I2 4-4-2 tank No. B14 is pictured with a London Bridge to Dorking North, via Mitcham Junction, train near Ewell East. No. B14 was one of ten 5ft. 6in. 4-4-2 tanks to be fitted with a slightly larger boiler than the Class I1 — a boiler that proved most successful on Col. L. Billinton's small 0-6-0 Class E2 tanks, but it was still too small for the duties required from the 4-4-2 tanks. The idea behind these two classes was correct. They were latterly stationed at Epsom in the mid-1920s for the suburban traffic, and could also be used on such fill-in duties during the day as the first class Pullman race train to, say, Gatwick. On Sundays, they could take empty suburban coaches to various South London stations, and then work excursions to Eastbourne, Brighton, Bognor, Littlehampton and even Portsmouth. They never minded travelling bunker first, so they were always immediately available for any duty. A typical Brighton suburban train of the 1920s is shown in this view — three R. J. Billinton 6 wheelers, four Brighton bogies and then three more 6 wheelers. D. Earle Marsh had come from Swindon to be H. Ivatt's second in command at Doncaster. He is reported not to have spoken to his chief at Swindon for several years, all necessary communication being by writing. At Swindon, he must have been involved with the enquiry into the derailment at speed of an express in Cornwall when it was being hauled by two 0-4-4 tank locomotives. Swindon dealt with this matter by changing the 0-4-4 tanks into 4-4-0s, after suplying them with tenders. Marsh went to Doncaster in 1897 and must have been associated with the LNER Class C12 4-4-2 tanks built that year. He was still at Doncaster when the 1903 Class R 0-8-2 suburban tanks were built. These proved overweight, and had to be rapidly fitted with much smaller boilers. On going to Brighton his first action was to remove the front coupling rods from several of Billinton's Class E4 and E5 0-6-2 tanks. I have never seen it stated why he had such a dislike of front-coupled locomotives. Perhaps it was possibly to do with the GWR derailment, or something to do with the 0-8-2 tanks, but this has never been made public. Finally, in 1908, an extremely successful superheated Class I3 4-4-2T was evolved. A superheater was a steam drier. Marsh was very knowledgeable on all Continental developments, and I was once informed by a Brighton official that Dr Schmidt himself came over to Brighton and personally set the valves of the LBSC 4-4-2 tanks, Nos. 22-26, which were described as 'wonder engines'. No. 24 was said to be the best, and was always used for the Royal train until its condition rapidly deteriorated after a collision at Streatham Junction in 1919. My informant added that 'Brighton was a small works and wished to take all the credit' — so Dr Schmidt was never afforded the praise he deserved. In 1909, No. 23 ran the 'Sunny South Express' working from Brighton through to Rugby, and back the next day, in competition with an LNWR 'Precursor' class 4-4-0. No. 23 ran so successfully, and with such economy of coal and water, that superheating quickly became established on all the main railways. The LNWR were so impressed with No. 23 that the superheated 'King George V' class 4-4-0s quickly followed *(Plate 63)*. Dr Schmidt is said to have visited Crewe Works, personally, to supervise their building. The only time the Class I3 4-4-2 tanks were regularly used bunker first on express duties was on bank holidays, when tremendous crowds would gather outside Brighton Station for the homeward journey. As soon as a train reached the London terminus, a Class I3 off the previous arrival would back on, having taken water, and would immediately return empty carriage stock to Brighton. In earlier days, on bank holiday excursions, it used to be the porters' duty at Three Bridges to remove 'dead drunks' from the train. Here they would be laid out on the platform and labelled with particulars of their return train. There was thus always plenty of time for drivers to take on all the water they needed while the porters were busy.

Plate 99: Class I3 superheated 4-4-2T No. 2091 climbs Falmer Bank. The class was completely adaptable and, with a water capacity of 2,100 gallon, could work the 11.35p.m. Victoria to Portsmouth express, which ran from Clapham Junction to Fratton; the longest Brighton non-stop run. I can remember on one occasion the 10.10a.m. from Victoria to Portsmouth was being badly delayed. The Midhurst branch train left Petworth after the Portsmouth train, but arrived in Chichester before it. The 10.10a.m. from Victoria was closely followed by the 11.35a.m. hauled by Class I3 4-4-2 No. 90, which stopped at Chichester Station to take water, even though the starting signal was off. The signalman wanted the driver of No. 90 to move up to the advanced starter at once and a tremendous argument ensued, the driver of No. 90 threatening to drop his fire — the water level on his tanks was so low. The two very elderly milk vans will be noted behind No. 2091.

Plate 100: An SR Class J2 4-6-2T, No. 2326, is pictured with an 'up' Eastbourne-Hayward's Heath-East Grinstead local train near Keymer Junction. Two of this type of locomotive were built. With a water capacity of just under 2,000 gallons (their original water capacity had been reduced to improve their steadiness) there was sometimes not much to spare on the 60 minute non-stop run from Victoria to Brighton. The other predominantly tank engine line, in addition to the LBSC, was the Lancashire & Yorkshire, but it was liberally supplied with water troughs. A Brighton fireman had to be very fit and agile, as all Brighton drivers liked to keep their tanks well topped up. The stop was made in a perfect position for the fireman to jump out, open the tank, get the bag into it and turn the water on, his driver always giving a helping hand. As soon as the guard waved his flag, the water would be turned off and the train would proceed to the next water column. At Cheam, water would always be taken while passengers were alighting and boarding the train. At most stations with water columns, there would always be some stately ladies sailing majestically up and down the platform looking for a lavatory carriage. A porter would be in attendance with their luggage — thus the driver usually had plenty of time to get all the water he needed. It was at this site that a relay station was being built for the Eastbourne electrification. These were the days before railway buses, and the builders were taken to and from the site by special train. One Saturday morning, when the General Manager, Sir Herbert Walker, was accompanying the train, the foreman found, on arrival at Hayward's Heath, that he had mislaid fifteen or so men. Sir Herbert Walker said, 'We must go back and find them'. They stopped at various possible places along the route and, finally, at the site shown in this photograph, Sir Herbert Walker heard a faint tapping noise and cries for help. He took the coal hammer off the engine and broke his way into the building to release the fifteen men. It is not reported what he said to his architect, on the Monday morning, for having forgotten about the door. This story is told in Sir Herbert Walker's biography — an excellent book.

Plate 101: The final Brighton line tank engine development was a 4-6-4 with a water capacity of nearly 2,700 gallons. This locomotive was introduced in 1914 to Col. L. Billinton's design. They were magnificent looking machines which settled down well after some teething troubles. This photograph shows SR Class L 4-6-4T No. 2328 on the 'down' 'City Limited' near Salfords Halt. The 'City Limited', the 4p.m. from London Bridge, was the crack businessman's commuter train to Brighton.

Plate 102: With the liberal Brighton loading gauge, there was little work for the class to do after the South Coast electrification, so the Class L tanks were altered to 4-6-0s and were used on the main line from Waterloo. In this view, one of these converted locomotives, SR 4-6-0 No. 2330 *Cudworth*, is seen working a 'down' Bournemouth express at Worting Junction.

Plate 103: In contrast to the SR Class L 4-6-4 tanks, were the small Class E1R 0-6-2Ts. Shown here is an SR Class E1R 0-6-2, No. 2124, entering Bideford with a Torrington train. The rear coach had been detached at Barnstaple off the 'Atlantic Coast Express'. No. 2124 was built by Stroudley at Brighton in 1878 as an 0-6-0T, and its boiler, cylinders, etc., were standard with his Class D1 0-4-2 tanks. They were free running locomotives in spite of their 4ft. 6in. driving wheels, and had performed a great deal of passenger work in their time. In 1928, ten, one of which was No. 2124, were altered to 0-6-2 tanks, and for nearly thirty years worked the Halwell Junction to Barnstaple branch, and also banked trains up the 1 in 37 incline from Exeter St. David's (the GWR Station) to Exeter Central. In 1924 there was a severe shortage of rolling stock and locomotives on the Southern Railway. The 8.10a.m. from Epsom was formed by stock which had been worked down empty from Eardley Sidings. When the train arrived at Victoria at 8.53a.m., it formed the 9.05a.m. to Brighton. On Saturdays, its formation was 7 Brighton balloon type bogies and 3 Pullmans cars (two on weekdays). The 8.10a.m. was rostered to be worked by an Epsom Class D1 0-4-2 tank. Epsom, at this time, had no spare engine so when an extra locomotive was necessary for boiler washouts, etc., Battersea would send down their yard pilot, Class E1 0-6-0T No. B606, and morning after morning this train of main line stock, hauled by a 50 year old Class D1 or E1 locomotive, would arrive punctually at Victoria, detrain all its suburban passengers (in those days everybody worked on Saturday mornings), entrain a platform full of passengers for Brighton, and be off again at 9.05a.m. The E1 0-6-0 tanks had a lever reverse. They would start off very fiercely in full gear, and then when they were notched up, speed fell off very rapidly. Then they would accelerate again with a jerk. Five of the Class E1R tanks on the Halwell Junction to Barnstaple duties had their wheels rebalanced, to give a smoother start.

Plate 104: In the 1923 railway Grouping, the Southern Railway absorbed the 19½ mile 1ft. 11½in. gauge light railway which ran between Lynton and Barnstaple, and ran it like a normal Southern Railway branch line. This picture shows ex-Lynton & Barnstaple 1ft. 11½in. gauge 2-6-2T No. 760 *Exe* shunting at Woody Bay. The signal is interesting, being of SR standard pattern, and made up of two old rails.

Plate 105: This shows the view from the footplate of SR ex-Lynton & Barnstaple 2-6-2T No. 759 *Yeo*, climbing a 1 in 40 gradient near Blackmoor. The driver was from Salisbury and, in the summer months, used to work on the main line between Salisbury and Exeter. During the winter I remember him telling me that he had put on a stone in weight.

Plate 106: When Stroudley died in 1889, his sucessor, R. J. Billinton, first cancelled an order which Stroudley had given for a further batch of Class D1 0-4-2 tank engines, and replaced them by a series of 0-4-4 tanks, very similar to those Johnson had been building at Derby. This photograph shows a Derby LMS 0-4-4 tank, No. 1260, built in 1876, with a Bletchley to Bedford railmotor train leaving Fenny Stratford. The coaches were fitted with very low steps, so that passengers could board the train easily from the platformless wayside halts. In summer these coaches would sometimes be used on a Yarmouth excursion. An LNWR 0-8-0 locomotive is being held at the signal.

Plate 107: An SR Class D3 0-4-4T, No. 2383, built in 1893, is seen with a 'down' train near Woldingham. When built, No. 383, with its tall Johnson chimney, and spring balance safety valves on the dome, bore a very strong resemblance to a Derby 0-4-4T. No. 383 was later fitted with the standard Marsh boiler and chimney, as shown in this photograph.

In 1891, Billinton completed a 4ft. 6in. 0-6-2T, which had originally been designed by Stroudley shortly before his death in 1889. He seems to have liked this locomotive as, in 1894, he built the first of a long series of 0-6-2 tanks, all fitted with 4ft. 3in. diameter standard boilers of the same basic measurements as Stroudley's prototype. The first series, Class E3 had, like Stroudley's engine, 4ft. 6in. driving wheels, and was intended for freight traffic. In 1897, they had been used so much for passenger traffic, being fitted with the Westinghouse brake, that the next batch, Class E4, was built with 5ft. driving wheels, and became real mixed traffic locomotives. On one occasion, in December 1934, Class J2 4-6-2T No. 2326 failed, with brake trouble, at Polegate on an 'up' Eastbourne express. Class E4 0-6-2T No. 2581 was shunting in the sidings and was immediately attached as pilot. She ran so well that she stayed on the train for the whole journey to Victoria. Class E4 0-6-2T No. 473 *Birch Grove* is fortunately being preserved in working order on the Bluebell Railway.

Plate 108: This shows SR Class E4 5ft. No. 2510 at the Dyke, Brighton; the train was composed of SECR, LSWR and LBSCR bogies. This was not a suburban rush hour train, as might be expected, but it was photographed on a Sunday afternoon. The passengers were going to walk on the South Downs. When the train was about to depart, the signalman would ring a bell which sounded in the bar of the Golf Club, which was situated beside the Golf Links Halt, on the way back to Brighton.

Plate 109: In 1903, there followed a series with 5ft. 6in driving wheels, as shown in this view featuring SR Class E5 0-6-2T No. B585. This class, and the very similar Class E6 0-6-2T which had 4ft. 6in. driving wheels, was of interest, as it always retained R. J. Billinton's chimney which was based on S. Johnson's Derby chimneys, which he first designed when he was Chief Mechanical Engineer of the GER at Stratford (London) between 1866 and 1873. No. B585 was working what was called 'The Managing Director's train'. It was the last of the rush hour trains into London Bridge, where it arrived about 10.45a.m., and was never heavily loaded. It ran non-stop from Three Bridges to East Croydon to the same timings as the 60 minute non-stop expresses from Brighton to London. A speed of 60m.p.h. always used to be attained in under two miles from the Three Bridges start, and a maximum of about 65m.p.h. was attained before starting the climb to Quarry Summit. It was this class of front-coupled tank engine that Marsh particularly disliked, and for a short time he removed their front coupling rods and relegated them for a time to minor duties. As soon as Marsh left Doncaster, H. A. Ivatt designed, in 1907, the very similar LNER Class N1 0-6-2 tank, which never gave any trouble and became the prototype of Sir Nigel Gresley's Class N2 suburban tanks, one of which is preserved at Loughborough. The LNER Class N2 0-6-2 tanks always required a good track.

In spite of the extensive electrification of the Central Section of the Southern Railway in the 1930s, relatively more Brighton locomotives survived into British Railways days, than either South Western or South Eastern. The Brighton line was essentially a suburban rather than main line railway. It had many race meetings, especially in May and June, and there were many school excursions into the countryside as well as to the seaside. Most of the locomotives for these trains had to stand about waiting for the return working later in the day.

It is interesting, when studying the old shed allocations, to note that New Cross locomotives always seemed to have a lower mileage than the others. It would seem that this shed was the standby for all the many specials.

Plate 110: Although Marsh only reboilered two of Stroudley's locomotives, he reboilered many of Billinton's small-boilered types with his standard 5ft. boiler. In this view an SR Class E5X rebuilt 0-6-2T, No. 2401, enters Dorking North on a local train from Horsham, and is composed of a two coach ex-LSWR railmotor set — a filling-in duty for No. 2401. The handrails round the dome were to assist the fireman when the locomotive had to take water. No. 2401 was one of four to be so rebuilt. It was a Horsham locomotive for nearly all of its existence, where it ran up a very high mileage. Before the Grouping, it was always employed on the days before and after bank holidays to work the second part of London to Portsmouth expresses — a long trip of 84 miles. R. J. Billinton's last class was similar to Class E5, but with 4ft. 6in. driving wheels for freight work.

Plate 111: An SR Class E6X 4ft. 6in. 0-6-2T, rebuilt with large standard boiler, is seen on a local freight train near Ewell East. The two E6X 0-6-2T locomotives were normally employed on the heavy cross-London coal trains. I only once saw one on a passenger train. With the building development of the 1920s, suburban freight trains were always well-loaded. Those were the days when the hoardings at every station would exhort passengers to 'Live in Surrey, free from worry', and 'Live in Kent and be content', to which, needless to say, the local wag always added 'Newly-weds should live in Beds.'.

Plate 112: This shows SR Class 0-6-4T, No. 1595, on a Tonbridge train, entering Oxted. This train was of interest in that it took the Crowhurst loop on to the Redhill to Tonbridge line. This loop was normally only used by one passenger train 'up' and 'down' a day, but it was a useful secondary route for hop-pickers' specials, etc., which could divert at Seldons Road on to the Elmer End branch. There were only five 0-6-4 tanks built. A series of ex-Midland Railway 0-6-4 tanks had to be withdrawn on account of their unsteadiness at speed.

Plate 113: In 1872, Johnson had built his first 0-4-4T for the GER, the basic design of which he took with him to Derby. This view shows LMS 0-4-4T No. 1346 entering Wells with a one coach train from Glastonbury, on the Somerset & Dorset Railway. The Great Western line from Witham to Yatton is shown between the two locomotives. The 0-6-0 locomotive is LMS No. 2882, a 1878 4ft. 6in. 0-6-0 designed by S. W. Johnson for the S&D Joint Railway.

Plate 114: In 1875, William Adams built a series of 0-4-4 tanks for the GER, similar to those of Samuel Johnson's 1872 design, but with 4ft. 10in. driving wheels. At Nine Elms, he built a large series of similar 4ft. 10in. locomotives for the LSWR, but with covered cabs. These were very long-lived and became well-known on account of their long sojourn on the Isle of Wight. This photograph shows one of these locomotives, SR 4ft. 10in. 0-4-4T No. 213, on the Weymouth to Easton branch. It was a pity that there was no colour film in those days. I have never forgotten climbing up the cliff, the massive white Portland rocks aflame with red valerian. Below lay the calm deep blue sea and above, the clear blue sky. The coaches were an interesting collection, converted from steam railmotor units.

Plate 115: A very difficult photograph to obtain was that of LMS 0-6-0T No. 1669, seen leaving Heath Park Halt, Hemel Hempstead. Most trains on the branch from Harpenden stopped at Hemel Hempstead, but there was one on Saturdays only which went through to Heath Park Halt at a time when a photograph was possible. No. 1669 is of interest in being Johnson's Derby design which, somewhat enlarged, became the standard London Midland Division's 'Jinty' 0-6-0T. The coach next to the locomotive was of S&D origin, and was still in its blue livery. The rear coach is an old Midland Railway clerestory.

Plate 116: An LMS 'Coal Tank', No. 7572, is pictured on a push and pull train at Uppingham. I can remember a wartime journey behind one of these locomotives from Craven Arms to Shrewsbury. LMS 2-6-4T No. 2404 had stalled on the bank up out of Swansea (St. Thomas), and had been banked by an LMS 0-6-0T locomotive, similar to that shown in the previous photograph. Later on, we had a ex-LNWR 0-8-0 engine as pilot up Sugar Loaf Mountain, and then, when passing two stations away from Craven Arms, the driver threw his old tobacco tin to the signalman asking for help. When we arrived the station pilot, a small 0-6-2T, similar to No. 7572, was waiting, having taken water, and there ensued a most exhilarating dash down to Shrewsbury, piloting the ailing No. 2404.

Plate 117: Before the advent of the LMS 2-6-4 tank, the Central Wales line was worked by Webb 5ft. 6in. 2-4-2 tanks, such as those shown in this view. This was an exceptionally long trip of over 100 miles for a small tank engine. Here we see 2-4-2T No. 6748 piloting LMS 2-4-2T No. 6652 on a train leaving Denbigh for Corwen. This was a lucky photograph, taken by chance when driving through the town. I never found out the details of the working.

Plate 118 (below): This shows an LMS 4ft. 6in. 2-4-2T, No. 6538, at Aylesbury with a train for Leighton Buzzard.

It was the Midland Railway who led the way in improving carriages, abolishing the second class in 1875. They introduced Pullman cars from America in the early 1870s.

During the 1920s and 1930s, first class Pullman race specials became very popular. A race-goer who lived near London could go to his office for an hour or two and then travel down to the racecourse in great comfort. Lunch would be served by his special steward. After the war, these specials never regained their popularity.

Plate 119 (top right): An SR Class J1 4-6-2T, No. B325, with a ten car 'down' 'Southern Belle' first and third Pullman train, is seen near Coulsdon. The 44 ton first class cars of 1908 were probably some of the most luxurious coaches built for every day use in England, but as they had been constructed for the very liberal Brighton loading gauge, their use after the Grouping was restricted, and they spent most of their latter years in Eardley carriage sidings. The train featured here would have weighed more than 400 tons, and had to be worked non-stop over the 50½ miles from Victoria to Brighton with a tank capacity of under 2,000 gallons. For a locomotive built in 1910, this was an excellent effort. The SR 'Schools' class 4-4-0s could run the 108 miles to Bournemouth without taking water, on 4,000 gallons, but they were twenty years younger.

Plate 120 (right): Another favourite Pullman train was the Sunday only 'Eastbourne Limited', shown in this view near Horley. It is being hauled by Class U1 3-cylinder 2-6-0 No. 1907. The middle coach is one of the 1908-built 'Southern Belle' cars. This was the last occasion that this train ran.

Plate 121: SR Class H15 4-6-0 No. 521 is pictured with the 'up' 'Bournemouth Belle' near Sway. It was unusual for a mixed traffic locomotive to work this train, although the load on that particular day was not heavy.

Plate 122: This shows SR Class H1 2041 *Peveril Point* with a 'down' Goodwood first class Pullman race special, near Christ's Hospital. It is believed that passengers on these trains were taken to the racecourse by bus from Chichester, and that the train did not go on to Singleton. In addition to the Pullman train, there was always one from London, composed of a 7 coach close-coupled Billinton set labelled 'Singleton'. This was always hauled by a B4 class 4-4-0, with straight backs to the seats and narrow compartments. The original third class coaches on these sets were acutely uncomfortable.

Plate 123: An SR Class H 0-4-4T, No. 1517 (pilot) and Class I3 4-4-2T No. 2921, haul a 'down' first class Pullman train from Victoria to Epsom Downs. On Derby Day 1935, these trains were so popular that two trains, one of eight cars and the other of nine cars, were run to Epsom Downs, and two trains of eight cars each were run to Tattenham Corner. Presumably, there were few Pullman cars on any boat train on Derby Day.

Plate 124: An LMS streamlined 4-cylinder 4-6-2, No. 6221 *Queen Elizabeth* heads the 'down' 'Coronation Scot' and takes water on Moore Troughs. From the photograph the streamlining does not appear to be very effective and it was removed after the war. The gathering storm clouds are clearly shown in this August 1939 scene. *Queen Elizabeth* was built in 1937 and this seems the perfect picture with which to end this book.

ABBREVIATIONS

LBSCR	London, Brighton & South Coast Railway
LSWR	London & South Western Railway
SECR	South Eastern & Chatham Railway
SER	South Eastern Railway
BR	British Railways
SR	Southern Railways
GWR	Great Western Railway
CLC	Cheshire Lines Committee
S&DJR	Somerset & Dorset Joint Railway
L&Y	Lancashire & Yorkshire Railway
NBR	North British Railway
CR	Caledonian Railway
K&ESR	Kent & East Sussex Railway
LMS	London, Midland & Scottish Railway
LNER	London & North Eastern Railway
G&SWR	Glasgow & South Western Railway
GER	Great Eastern Railway
LT&SR	London, Tilbury & Southend Railway
PD&SWJ	Plymouth, Devonport & South Western Junction Railway
M&GN	Midland & Great Northern Railway

Southern Railway Numbering:
From 1923-32 the pre-grouping LSWR numbers remained as before.
The SECR locomotives had an 'A' prefix (Ashford).
The LBSC locomotives had a 'B' prefix (Brighton).

In 1932 the Ashford locomotives had 1000 added to their numbers.
  the Brighton locomotives had 2000 added to their numbers.
  the duplicate LSWR locomotives had 3000 added to their numbers (the capital list numbers remaining as in LSWR days).

In 1948, under British Railways, the Southern locomotives had 30000 added to their 1932 numbers. A few ex-works locomotives in the first couple of months, had their 1932 numbers prefixed by an 'S'.